Around & A

TAVISTOCK

Chips Barber

Best wishes!

Chips Barber

OBELISK PUBLICATIONS

Also by the Author

Diary of a Dartmoor Walker
Diary of a Devonshire Walker
Ten Family Walks on Dartmoor
Ten Family Walks in East Devon
Six Short Pub Walks on Dartmoor
The Great Little Dartmoor Book
The Great Little Chagford Book
Beautiful Dartmoor
Dark and Dastardly Dartmoor
Weird and Wonderful Dartmoor
Cranmere Pool – The First Dartmoor Letterbox
The Teign Valley of Yesteryear, Parts I and II
Princetown of Yesteryear, Parts I and II
Widecombe – A Visitor's Guide
Railways on and around Dartmoor
Along The Tavy
Around & About Roborough Down

Other Dartmoor Titles

The Great Walks of Dartmoor, Terry Bound
The A to Z of Dartmoor Tors, Terry Bound
Walks in the Chagford Countryside, Terry Bound
Walks in the Shadow of Dartmoor, Denis McCallum
Walks in Tamar and Tavy Country, Denis McCallum
The Templer Way, Derek Beavis
The Dartmoor Mountain Bike Guide, Peter Barnes
Wheelchair Walks in Devon, Lucinda Ruth Gardner
Circular Walks on Eastern Dartmoor, Liz Jones
Under Sail Through South Devon and Dartmoor, Raymond B. Cattell

We have over 150 Devon titles. For a full list of current books, please contact us at Obelisk Publications, 2 Church Hill, Pinhoe, Exeter, Devon, EX4 9ER or telephone (01392) 468556.

Acknowledgements

Thanks to the following people for their help: Mr Stacey (Creber's), Susan Cadogan-Smith at Bedford Hotel, Carolyn Wixon of Tavistock TIC, Chris Foote, Dave Davies and M. R. Stacey.

First published in 1998 by
Obelisk Publications, 2 Church Hill, Pinhoe, Exeter, Devon
Designed by Chips and Sally Barber
Typeset by Sally Barber
Printed in Great Britain by
The Devonshire Press, Torquay, Devon

TAVISTOCK

"Tavistock is the most delightful town in West Devon", wrote the late Professor W. G. Hoskins, a man who knew the history and setting of a thousand towns throughout the British Isles. And few would argue against him, because Tavistock has an air about it which draws visitors back, time and time again, and encourages many others to want to settle or remain here.

However, there was a time when to come from, or even trade out of, Tavistock was regarded with a degree of contempt by neighbouring communities. This was written by H. Sharrock on 29 December 1883:

"It is a fact that a horse dealer has been known to abate a seller's price, by some pounds, with the remark that the pony would be a good one but for having 'Tavistock Legs'. In this usage of the name the first syllable is pronounced with a contemptuous emphasis. Now Tavistock has nothing visibly contemptible about it, being a town of fair site, of convenient habitation, of ancient good fame, the birthplace of Sir Francis Drake and other worthies... A certain man of Tavistock was asked if he could account for the general disparagement affected by the neighbours from Okehampton to Plymouth. His answer was concise 'They'm jealous'."

Raymond B. Cattell followed the same tack in his wonderful 1930s book *Under Sail Through Red Devon*, where he had this to say of the prowess of Tavistock folk: *"No man who visits the West Country should permit himself to be baulked of viewing sturdy, granite Tavistock, embowered in her woods and preserving still the spirit of her sons – Drake, William Browne, mellowest of Elizabethan poets, Capt Rich-Peake and many other individuals of strong personality and reckless courage.*

Tavistock has a reputation among Devonians of being a kind of wild, untamable Far West, where men are men and life insurance is high. Still, today, one of its chief exports is of he-men for the less civilised parts of the Empire. One of these, who was a great friend of mine, having given me a black eye when we were both small boys, found the sheriffs of America too interfering and Mexico too civilised. The wilder parts of Australia staved off boredom for a time, but in the end he was compelled to come back to Tavistock to be in the company he loved. His lightning lasso is the wonder of all who have to round up moorland cattle and his capacity for liquor is a subject of sermons.

Briton, Roman, Irishman, Saxon and Dane have fought over the jewel that is Tavistock, and it is not surprising if the survivors are a little tough. In 997, thirty years after Buckland Abbey had been built, the Danes took Tavistock, burnt the Minster, and retired with much booty, to the great chagrin of the reigning monarch, Ethelred the Unready. Next came Irishmen from Kerry, as witness those runic stones in the present vicarage garden. One of these saints built an abbey, which has lately been shamelessly pulled down to make way for a pub...

Typical of Tavistock is that Rich-Peake who sailed from Plymouth and started a purely individual invasion of Spain. Wandering far from his ship among orange groves, he met a richly apparelled Spanish knight, Don Juan of Cadiz, and after defeating him in a single combat, chivalrously spared his life and allowed him to retire. This worthy sent back two dozen musketeers who took Rich-Peake prisoner and treated him grievously, upon which the Tavistock man sadly reflects, 'True Valour (I see) goes not aluaies in good Clothes, for Don Juan (when my hands were bound) wounded me through the Face from Eare to Eare.' Later he was threatened with torture by the Duke of Medina, who wanted information about the English fleet, and finally was set to fight for his life against Spanish challengers. He, however, disposed of the first two so quickly that the rest of the list was called in vain, whilst the king, greatly impressed, secured him for his bodyguard. Years later he returned to be a respected churchwarden at Tavistock...

...For my part I like Tavistock men, whether they shoot sheriffs or linger over love lyrics, but it cannot be denied that, as one good Devonian has said, 'There was and is an ancient prejudice against men of Tavistock. In Tavistock it is ascribed to jealousy. Outside Tavistock they do not attempt to explain, but act upon it, with the promptness of three Okehampton men who, seeing a pedlar struggling in a flooded brook which was washing him away, were about to help him out, when one said: 'Augh, tes only a Tavistock man, let'n goo!' Which they accordingly did without much remorse.

...Tavistock's women were true matches for their husbands, as is witnessed by Lady Howard, 'the female bluebeard', a clever but reckless woman – one of the brightest in all the pack of 'cards' which Tavistock has produced. I will say no more of her, for her ghost still drives in the coach which rumbles from Fitzford House up to the moors, every night at one o'clock – and I wish to spend my nights on the moors with no more ghosts than are absolutely necessary."

In *My Devonshire Book*, published in 1907 by J. Henry Harris, he has this to say of the same story: *"If repetition can make a story true, this IS true. It has been told and sung to every tune that will suit a ballad for centuries. It has been handed down as an article of belief by people who have seen the ghostly lady enter her carriage of bones, drawn by skeleton horses, driven by a skeleton coachman, and preceded by a coal-black hound with eyes of flashing fire. Generations of Tavistock men have shuddered at the thought of passing Fitzford Gateway at midnight for fear of meeting the coal-black hound and carriage of bones and the ghostly lady. Isn't there some Society to take the matter up?"* Tavistock has therefore rubbed shoulders with the titled, talented, brave, benevolent, rich, rugged, foolish, famous and notorious.

But so far we have ignored some of the fundamental points as to why a town developed here at Tavistock at all. Arthur Mee summed it up like this in his 1930s book, in 'The King's England' series, *Devon: "It is believed that Tavistock is one of the older parts of Devon to be peopled, prehistoric settlers having been drawn to it by the good supplies of tin found on the surface. It comes into history a hundred years before the Conqueror, having apparently been a military post on the River Tavy. What we know of it begins with the building of its Abbey, a rich centre of religious life founded by Ordgar, whose daughter had been married to King Edgar, nephew of the first king of all England, Athelstan. There was little peace in those days, and in 16 years the Danes destroyed the abbey, but it was built again by Ordgar's son Ordulph, and soon became a place of high renown and influence in the town. In the jubilee year of the Norman Conquest Tavistock received a charter and became a market town, and it was governed from the abbey till 1539 when Henry VIII broke up the monasteries and gave the estates to his friends. Tavistock Abbey was given to John Russell, first Earl of Bedford. By this time the trade in wool had brought the town new life and prosperity, and its manufacturers had secured the sole rights to make certain woollen cloths called Tavistocks. In the Civil War [1642–1646] the town was held for Parliament by the Earl of Bedford, but changed hands six times.*

The stones of the old abbey still left for us to see are in the heart of the town round the great square laid out by Duke Francis, who spent his mining royalties in developing the town. He cleared away its narrow streets and laid out this square with wide streets running off; it is one of the most attractive spaces in the heart of any Devon town, with a fine old church, town hall, the hotel, the central market, and a handsome block of buildings all doing their best to preserve the dignity of town with so fine a past. Here, too, is the river, with the ruined walls of the abbey on its banks."

One of town's pubs is the Ordulph Arms which, without a local history lesson, might appear to be an unusual choice of name. This is a building that has been constructed, apparently, with stones from the former Tavistock Abbey, originally rebuilt by Ordulph. I wonder what he would have made of such a secular building as a pub being named after him so many centuries later? Prior to this most recent of names it honoured another local hero, Sir Francis Drake. As is so common in life, little stays the same for long and this pub's building has also been the Rural District Offices, and Shepherd's Temperance and Commercial Hotel. I wonder what next?

We have mentioned just a handful of the more famous people with a Tavistock connection and could mention the likes of others with strong connections by birth, marriage, death or circumstance like Mrs Bray, William Browne, Andy Hicks, Michael Heseltine, Angela Rippon, Phil de Glanville, Clive Gunnell and so on, but for now they will have to wait for another volume, because it's time to consider an event that has put the town firmly on the map...

As a complete outsider I am not really sure what to make of the celebrated Tavistock Goose Fair because I have only been twice: once as a small child, when I only have the vague recollections of splashing through puddles, munching a toffee apple and becoming 'face-caked' in candy floss, and once as an adult, when I managed to avoid similar discomforts. As I was a teacher in East Devon for some twenty years, Goose Fair always coincided with a school day when I was obliged to be at the 'chalk-face', so it was only after a major career change that the opportunity arose to go again. Some folks love this sort of event and others don't, and it's definitely a case of, "What's good for the goose isn't always good for the Tavistock gander!" I must confess that I didn't go to have a good time or to become involved in the event; my quest was simple – I needed to take a colourful photograph for the cover of this book and, perhaps, make a few useful contacts for furthering my research.

I have heard that there is a certain magnetism that draws people to Goose Fair time and time again. In my 'middle age' I know that even if I caught the fair bug I would never be able to match the feat of Harry Clemens; in 1965 this former Tavistock saddler, who had retired to Sticker in Cornwall, made his 71st consecutive visit at the age of 91.

In planning my visit I contacted Tavistock's excellent Tourist Information Centre for advice on parking for the event and was informed that it would be most sensible to use the 'park and ride' facility specially set up away from the town centre. However, I opted for a 'park and walk' from a car park on Whitchurch Down just south-east of 'the Pimple'.

There is a terrific view from the Pimple and it had been a few years since I last visited this superb vantage point, rising above the general level of the golf course, with views all around. The distant hills of Bodmin Moor, Kit Hill and the closer-to-home Dartmoor alps make for a wonderful landscape. The Pimple's crowning building was designed, I believe, by the eminent architect Sir Edwin Lutyens, who was also responsible for the Cenotaph in London, Castle Drogo, near Drewsteignton, and the Drum Inn at Cockington.

This beauty 'spot' was the scene of a much-talked-about incident about a century ago, when a well-known character, Alfy Jordan, had his patience sorely tested. He had, for a nominal sum, agreed to push a local man, in a wheelchair, from the town all the way to this high point. However,

the journey became a real ordeal for poor Alfy. The gradients he could manage; the weight of the wheelchair occupant was also no problem. What really got to him was the fact that his client, who was a deeply religious man, continually pointed out Alfy's spiritual shortcomings as they scaled the hill. Alfy  needed to bring relief to his bible-bashed ears so, when they reached the Pimple, he applied the brake and left his charge alone to reflect on the ways of the Lord. How long he had to wait before being discovered and taken back to Tavistock, I do not know, but I trust he had the good sense to keep quiet on the return journey!

Poor Alfy's life ended when he drowned in the River Tavy in the winter of 1922.

With this story in my mind, I descended the not quite so righteous path from the Down towards the town. Having assumed that cars wouldn't have been allowed into Tavistock, it was quite a surprise to see the road from the golf club to the town an unbroken line of parked vehicles.

I wasn't naive enough to imagine that Goose Fair would still be dominated by geese, or other forms of animal, brought to town to be sold. And, indeed, the only 'animals', in the heart of Tavistock, were the cuddly toys on the various stalls and game booths. In order to acclimatise to the enormous crowds that I had heard would soon swamp Tavistock, I got there just after 9.00 a.m., and at that time there were more stallholders than spectators. Those traders, blessed with the 'gift of the gab', were strangely silent, but perhaps they were holding themselves back for some real vocal action later, when the masses arrived.

In my mind I had pictured a handful of fairground rides and stalls in Bedford Square, and they were there, but it had never occurred to me that the entire length of the extremely long Plymouth Road, from Bedford Square to Drake's Statue, would be one continuous line of stalls, rides and fair-day attractions. Originally the stalls had run along Whitchurch Road, but from 1973 Plymouth Road had become the preferred option for expanding the Fair.

Goose dinners being promoted at a Goose Fair of yesteryear

Having been stuck here in gloom-and-doom traffic jams, on past occasions, it was an astonishing contrast to see it looking so colourful, a scene of intense pedestrian activity. The hardened, seasoned traders, whose life evolves around events like these, had their game plan, knew the score and obviously anticipated a prosperous Goose Fair.

However, in the past the behind-the-scenes preparations were not always that smooth. Just getting to or from the fair was no easy matter for some of the heavier attractions. Before the First World War Hancock's Fair, travelling from their home base in Plymouth, had their stalls and booths pulled by teams of horses. On the heavier items eight sturdy steeds were required to pull them up the steep hills along the way. Going downhill was also a testing time and poles were carried and used as 'brakes' to wedge beneath the turning wheels. When Whiteleggs first started bringing traction engines to Goose Fair it took them a day to travel the twelve miles from Plymouth.

The fair, always appearing to evolve away from the original agricultural event, must have been an even more colourful occasion when the likes of the boxing booths, sword swallowers, and fire eaters entertained and excited the crowds, at a time when people were much more easily impressed by less sophisticated pleasures than they are today.

Television companies, handily placed in Plymouth to reach Tavistock, and local radio stations, usually cover the event. As they prepared for 'action', with their early morning briefing, the town quickly began to fill, the tide of humanity being only one way and that incoming. The media were well represented. Film crews (and radio interviewers) were out and about trying to get enough 'footage' to make an attractive segment for their evening programmes. Each year they look for a new angle on covering the same event. Seeing them reminded me of the time when *Spotlight*, BBC's early evening regional news and magazine programme, looked at this event through the eyes of a giant goose. Former presenter Chris Denham had the unenviable task of donning a goose costume and, in the company of the always colourful Tony Beard, alias 'the Widecombe Wag', travelling around the town to the strains of the now traditional 'Tavvystock Goozey Vair' song. The words (which are included later) and music were penned by C. John Trythall in 1912.

Years ago, in the pre-mass-media age, Goose Fair entertained many hundreds of sailors from the Plymouth area and one might argue whether it was the culture or the all day drinking that drew them here. To facilitate their speedy removal from the pubs, all the doors were taken off their hinges. In those now long-gone days this side of the event was sometimes a much too boisterous one. The White Hart was once wrecked by drunken revellers, an episode that made most of the local landlords feel 'enough was enough'. However, on a lighter note, it was regarded as a bit of fun to see 'what became of the drunken sailors', not early in the morning but late in the evening when they had to return to their ships or bases. Inevitably when they most needed their faculties these often deserted them. Tavistock had two stations,

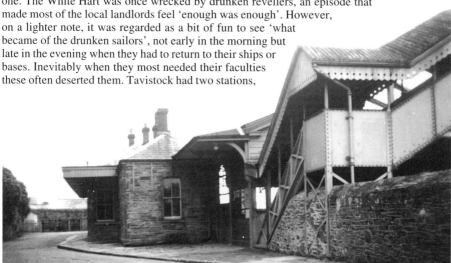

Tavistock South, now long gone, in one of its quieter moments

North and South, and although these were on two separate lines, it was possible to get to Plymouth from either. It was also possible to 'accidentally' head in the opposite direction and many did, ending up in either Launceston or Exeter. Some of the local townsfolk liked to see their departure, a frenzy of fisticuffs, and some sad and sorry sights, scenes regarded by some as great anthropological entertainment.

I walked the length of Plymouth Road, a broad nineteenth century thoroughfare which had, in 1960, been adapted on fair day as a car park, as other parking facilities to accommodate those driving to the event had reached saturation. Today, however, it was a traffic no-go area, this being the principal street for trading. At the street's western end stood Drake, as depicted by Boehm's statue, just a short distance from his birthplace. What would he have made of all this? The old picture postcard view (opposite) was taken before Drake Villas were built beyond it.

What would make a good cover for a book? Today there were no drunken sailors in uniform, nor television presenters dressed as geese, to make an eye-catching cover picture. What was required was something that was colourful, allowed enough space for the title at the top and said "Tavistock" with its town centre buildings. It had been cloudy all morning but there had been a few chinks in the sea of grey cloud and a large patch of blue, enough 'to make a sober sailor's pair of trousers', was approaching but would it last long enough for that one perfect picture to be taken? The sunlight was now illuminating the nearby hills and soon the dull day would be ablaze with colour. With a loaded camera and an estimated half an hour of the best quality light, at most,

there would be no time to lose as the clouds rolled back and the sun burst forth. The balloon seller, with his colourful collection of assorted, inflated shapes, added colour to the foreground (or was it fairground?) but the fair-goers, now passing by in greater numbers, made it hard to frame a suitable shot. In a mild panic, and quickly weighing up the situation, I saw the place for the best and most photogenic view would have to be the roof of the Bedford Hotel.

This is a green Hurdwick stone building, erected in 1720 by Jacob Saunders, standing on land once occupied by Tavistock Abbey. The hotel was built to be the private residence of the Duke of Bedford's steward, and following this it was a vicar's impressive residence. It became a hotel in 1822, John Truscott becoming the first occupier. It once had a fine ballroom, the work of the famous Plymouth architect John Foulston. Alas, priorities, in the early 1950s, dictated that more bedrooms were necessary. And so the colourful Hunt balls and dances staged there gave way in the conversion, when the ballroom was turned into two tiers of bedrooms.

Many guests have passed through its portal down the years. This was part of an entry written in the whimsical *Tour of North Devon*, published in 1887: "*Tavistock reached we had little difficulty in finding good quarters for man and beast at the Bedford Hotel. Clean and pretty Tavistock looked as fresh as a vestal virgin; and as we drove into the Bedford yard the bells struck out a merry peal. How they knew we were coming we never could find out...*

One visitor only, besides ourselves, invaded the coffee-room and as he seemed to be a stranger, we naturally asked him what he thought of Tavistock. He opened his eyes very wide, as he was evidently an Englishman, we daresay he was surprised that anyone should speak to him as we had done. After looking around and somewhat recovering his equanimity, he said he thought Tavistock the funniest place he was ever in, for at daybreak that morning he had been awoke by the bells

chiming 'Auld Lang Syne' just at a moment when he did not wish to remember anything."

I fully expected to be refused, at the hotel's reception desk, when I asked if I could climb up on to the roof to take some photographs but a Guardian Angel, in the form of the manageress, was most helpful even though she was under considerable pressure. For all the staff this was a busy day in a full-to-overflowing hotel. In this maelstrom of activity I was chaperoned to a door, smaller than the size of a window, that led onto the irregular-shaped roof, invisible to passers-by in the street, behind the rooftop crenellations. A blanket of grey sky was now only minutes away as I carefully tiptoed along the channels between the serrated roof ridges. Below was the scene that said it all, 'Tavistock', with its impressive Bedford Square AND its Goosie Fair in one shot. It wasn't every day that such a superb photo-opportunity presented itself. Having exhausted that view, with several shots, I noticed that there were even higher parts of the roof, so temporarily put my acrophobia, hypsophobia or even plain cremnophobia on hold and climbed higher to the top of the building. Whilst on the highest point I noticed a sign, on the even higher church tower opposite, saying something like '50 pence to climb the tower', which stirred some more thoughts. Despite knowing that certain obstructions in the line of view would not give me any better picture from there, it was yet another opportunity which I felt I shouldn't miss. The sky was still blue, the adrenaline in full flow.

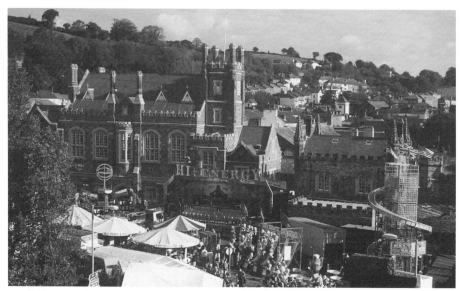

I carefully inched my way back to the point where I had climbed out onto the roof and was surprised, then shocked, to find the opening closed and bolted! The sheer brilliance of the sunlight made it difficult to see in. The next several minutes were passed with a continual tapping on the window, in the hope that I could attract somebody's attention to let me in. It was only when it became overcast that I realised I was looking in from above a deep stair-well! I had tried to enter the wrong opening; the 'door' I needed was on the other side of the building, which I soon located. What a fool! Fortunately nobody else had been privy to this fiasco, so I said 'thank you' to the staff in reception and left the Bedford Hotel, glad to be just stupid rather than maimed.

The best place to repent one's stupidity was the nearby parish church and the modest entrance fee proved a worthwhile investment. I was glad that it was not Midsummer's Eve, because one of the superstitions attached to this church once had an unfortunate finale, in the seventeenth century, for two Tavistock brothers. It was an annual custom of morbid curiosity to peer through the keyhole of the church in the belief that it was possible to see the spirits of those unfortunate folk who were scheduled to die in the coming year. The brothers peered in and, horror of horrors, saw themselves enter the door at the far end. Sure enough, they weren't there the following year to see the next phantom preview!

I was told that there were 114 steps to the the top of the narrow spiral staircase, which becomes still narrower the higher one climbs. On the way up there is a room with all the ropes for the bells, and the certificates gained by accomplished teams of ringers at the church. I briefly pondered over whether these bells tolled for the unfortunate Rev H. G. Le Neveu, an elderly Tavistock vicar who, in October 1917, was killed when was he was knocked down by a bicycle on a visit to Surbiton

in London. They certainly were rung all day when the railway arrived on a fine summer's day in June 1859. The bells, weighing a total of four tons, were first cast in 1769 by Thomas Bilbie of Cullompton, where there is a road named in his honour. They were recast and rehung in 1925 by John Taylor of Loughborough.

The bells looked impressive, but to a non-campanological mind were nothing compared to the view all over and around the town. Far below was the ever-busy Bedford Square and for those who love Gothic-styled buildings this run of edifices will please them. From this height the statue of the seventh Duke of Bedford, the work of Exeter sculptor Edward Bowring Stephens, and cast in metals mined from this district in 1864, looked very small indeed. The sculpted presence of the Duke, in 'his' Square, is most fitting. He was instrumental in the building changes in the heart of Tavistock in the mid-nineteenth century, funded largely from the profits made in the Tamar Valley copper mines. In the place of slums fine civic buildings arose, including a new Pannier Market and a line of buildings on the south side of Duke Street. This thoroughfare is aptly named because Tavistock is a town that owes its early history, as we have seen, to the former Tavistock Abbey and its later development to the Dukes of Bedford. However, the ducal fortunes saw a decline just before the First World War, when the eleventh Duke of Bedford felt obliged to sell the lion's share of his properties in the town.

The granite setts or cobbles either side of the gateway leading to Tavistock's Pannier Market, invisible from the height of the tower and beneath the various rides and stalls, blend in with many of the other granite stones used around the town. However, although most of this durable rock has been brought the short distance from nearby Dartmoor, these cobbles came all the way from Portugal, 700 miles as the crow flies. The art of making the setts had passed into the realms of folklore and the London agent, acting in 1976, saw this as a sensible solution to meet the town's requirements. Perhaps this is Tavistock's equivalent of 'taking coals to Newcastle'.

Panning around the 360 degree view, many landmarks could be spotted, particularly the enormous railway viaduct and the remarkable and enormous Fitzford Church, one of only two in the entire country to have a Lombardo-Venetian tower. It's strange how staring at a view can revive memories of one's youth. It has been many years since I was a fresh-faced youngster traipsing, under the enormous weight of a heavily laden rucksack, into Tavistock. With friends we laid our heads

down at the Youth Hostel at Abbotsfield Hall. I didn't know then that Dwight D. Eisenhower had been here, not that many more years before our visit in the mid-'60s. There is a plaque stating that he and Field Marshal Montgomery held several important meetings here prior to the D-Day landings in 1944. This building was the HQ of the 29th Infantry Division of the US Army.

Looking around this serene landscape, even with the Goose Fair in full swing, it was hard to believe that crucial decisions and planning, which have ultimately affected all our lives, one way or another, should have taken place here. It is now a nursing home.

By now enough pictures had been taken and on returning 'back to earth' it was obvious that the crowds were going to be almost stifling as Plymouth Road was a sea of bodies, of all shapes, sizes and ages.

Hidden from view was Betsy Grimbal's Tower, where legend has it that an unfortunate girl of this name was a Goose Girl. She was supposedly murdered by a soldier and is said still to haunt these environs, but on this particular Goose Fair Day she wasn't to be seen!

The salesmen were now in full cry and the air filled with pop music and the smell of hot doughnuts, hot dogs and onions. The large car park at the Wharf was completely covered in rides and fairground stalls, an incredible sight. For a while I ducked, rather than 'goosed', away from the revelry, opting to have a quick 'gander' at the stalls inside the Pannier Market. I had heard that the problems of too many pigeons in this building had led to the placement of stuffed predatory birds and high in the window was a creature bound to strike fear and trepidation into the hearts of 'the enemy', or so it was thought. This building is popular with shoppers and visitors because there is the surprise element of not knowing what sort of items might be 'up for grabs', not the run-of-the-mill merchandise normally found in the more predictable 'High Street' chain stores.

Not many will look down at the granite floor but, for those who know and love their native Dartmoor, they might like to know that this granite was hewn from Pew or Pu Tor, just under three miles due east of the town. This tor is one of the few to have been 'bombed' during the war when German planes dumped surplus explosives. Although no people were harmed, several Dartmoor ponies were killed.

Having browsed around the great variety of stalls, I headed back into the fray which was now Bedford Square at its peak of people-packedness; considering the almost non-appearance of geese, perhaps the event should be renamed 'Tavistock Sardine Fair'!

However, there was a real threat of rain in the air, in a town that enjoys more than its fair share of precipitation, so it was time to leave the revellers behind and take a look at the reason why Goose Fair became such an important date on the Dartmoor calendar. This was the animal side of the event, one that now seems to play a supporting role in the proceedings.

The Cattle Market was smaller than I had expected and the auction room was so crowded that even the 'sardines' in Bedford Square would have felt uncomfortable in such tightly-packed conditions. I had hoped to talk to someone who might have remembered auctioneer Tom Brown, who did this fast-talking job for a staggering 50 years but, understandably, everyone was preoccupied.

Outside in a nearby shed there were geese in pens, and in a much more relaxed atmosphere spectators looked on them with such intense curiosity that they might just as well have been caged Martians. The ancestors of these geese would have been walked to market, often setting out in the middle of the night to be escorted along the lanes leading to Tavistock. There was always a 'pecking order' in those yesteryear fair days when the time of arrival was all important. Experienced folk knew only too well that certain pens of animals would come up for sale at prime times when the bidding was keenest. This led to some extraordinary journeys. Dinah Tuckett, in those days of yore, carried a storm lamp as she left her farm, Dunnabridge (between Two Bridges and Dartmeet), in the midnight hour to walk the many miles to Tavistock with her geese, but she knew it was a worthwhile nocturnal exercise in order to get the best pens. She would probably have been less than happy to learn that in  1956 geese would effectively be banned from the Goose Fair, and not reappear until 1967. Regulations had been introduced to stop the movement of such birds to market after 30 September each year, to arrest the spread of fowl pest across the country.

The origins of the Fair, of which there are various theories, go back a long way and are somewhat shrouded in the mists of time, where detail is hazy. It's believed the Festival of St Michael or Michaelmas, a September event, was traditionally a time when roast goose was served up as it was a prime time for 'marketing' these poor creatures. It was also the time when the Goose Fair used to be held, that is up to the shift to the Gregorian calendar in 1752, when the Fair's fixed date moved from 29 September to 10 October, this remaining the case until 1822. It was then decided to plump for the second Wednesday in October, on which it remains to this day.

There is another school of thought that says the Abbey, whose patron was St Rumon, was granted a charter, in 1116, to hold a three-day fair to celebrate him. During this event it became something of a norm for those who owed monies to the Abbey to settle up. It was not unusual for debts to be paid in kind and the Abbey, no doubt, collected quite a gigantic gaggle of geese. They, in turn, needed a later occasion to offload their surplus stock, this being the Goose Fair which supplanted St Rumon's Fair. There is an old rhyme which goes back to at least 1575, or maybe even earlier, that went something like this: "When the tenants come to pay their quarter's rent, They bring a goose at Michaelmas and a dish of fish in Lent." Nottingham also has an important Goose Fair.

Others say that Goose Fair's title is a corruption from the name of the parish church, this being St Eustace or Eustachius.

This appeared in William Crossing's *The Western Gate of Dartmoor – Tavistock and its Surroundings*, in 1903: *"The two principal fairs are held on the second Wednesday in September and October. The former is known as 'Jan's Fair' and the latter, in which amusement forms a large element, as 'Joan's Fair'. On this occasion the bird that was once said to be 'Too much for one and not enough for two' is greatly in evidence, which has caused this holiday to be also widely known as 'Goose Fair'."*

Climbing, but not 'goose-stepping', back up to Whitchurch Down is always sobering exercise.

Down Road was still a long line of parked cars, their occupants obviously intent on making a real day of it. Where the road kinked I paused to "Rest and Remember Edward W. Chilcott, Good Cricketer, Good Citizen, Good Friend, September 1931", whose simple but touching memorial lies at the bottom of the slope leading up to the open Down.

Even from the heights above the cricket ground it was possible to hear all the merriment going on below, but by the time the Pimple had been conquered again, via the precipitous west face, the sounds of the fair had died away. For me the Goosie Fair was over but for thousands of others it had only just begun, and many would revel their way through the rest of the day and well into the night. It's not just an annual event but is a major regional occasion which will mean different things to different people, a vibrant day when the town is full of people intent on having a great day out, and one that certainly helps to keep the town's name firmly on the map.

By now those creatures of the common, the golfers, had emerged in force and had spaced themselves out fairly evenly across Whitchurch Down. Tavistock folk have enjoyed this royal and ancient game since the course began to evolve in 1890. It was created on land of heather, gorse and bracken, formerly owned by the Duke of Bedford, and perfectly suited for this game. It is said that the idea came from the aptly-named J. R. Divett, of the Royal North Devon, and its date makes it the second oldest surviving course in the county. Nature would appear to be the best groundsman, or is it greenkeeper? The generous rainfall, the grazing animals and the moorland turf have all played their part in making this an easier course to manage than many of the more recently engineered, cunningly calculated courses found springing up in other locations throughout the length and breadth of the kingdom.

But what is it they say about the best-laid plans of mice and men, and sometimes ponies? One might have thought that the practice putting green within the safe confines of the clubhouse grounds would have been safe from damage. However this wasn't the case, some years ago, for members and officials were strangely perplexed to find their wonderful surface was somewhat less perfect than it should have been. What was the cause of the problem?

Some of the club's officials, late one night, discovered that moorland ponies were the culprits, having worked out how to negotiate a self-latching gate. The solution was simple. Put a padlock on it and not even the most Houdini-like ponies could pick that. End of problem? No: still the ponies persisted in their quest to reach the putting area. Another nocturnal vigil answered a question that had bemused many members who simply could not fathom how any creature could breach such an animal-proof area. Those who saw it must have been quite dumbfounded to see a pony approach the small cattle grid at the entrance. No, it didn't take a run up and long-jump the obstacle; it was far too canny for that. The pony lay down beside it and just rolled over, spreading the girth of its body and the length of its legs which were longer, in total, than the width of the grid. Who says animals are not intelligent?

The 'sport of kings' was, in the early part of the nineteenth century, much in evidence. Rachel Evans had the pleasure of visiting the races on Whitchurch Down which, by the time she put pen to paper in 1846, had already become a thing of the past. This is what she saw, on a day when it didn't rain and before the greater or lesser golfer had become a naturalised species here! *"Our carriage has since rolled over the same soft turf, but on a far different occasion. The glare of the day then revealed a busy multitude of gay attire; collected to enjoy the exciting sport of horse racing. The hum of voices rose merrily on our ear, mingled with loud shouts of laughter, and the neighing of impatient steeds. Vociferous cries of the 'names, weights and colours of the riders' intruded on our attention; ballad singers bawled their loudest ditties to the listening rustics; our old friends Punch and Judy fought and chattered as loudly as ever, while a band of musicians played our national airs amidst the continually increasing din and uproar. Vehicles of all descriptions lined the sides of the course; booths with gay streamers denoted the vicinity of good cheer, while a handsome stand protected the charms of a number of ladies from the powerful rays of a noon-day sun..."* Rachel described the excitement of a race, in her own inimitable style, and then finished by saying that: *"It is not likely that the turfy slopes of Whitchurch Down will ever more resound to the shouts of the victorious jockey, or be the tavern or gambling house; but the playful colts fling their manes in the air, and bound over the shaven course at liberty; may they long be preserved from the fate of 'the high-mettled racer' made food for the hounds! The late Duke of Bedford who once subscribed to the races, transferred his handsome donation to an Agricultural society recently established in Tavistock."*

My more than modest vehicle, which I had left several hours earlier, was safely regained, and this as the heavens opened and a Dartmoor downpour duly commenced.

If you are one of those people who say "Goose Fair isn't what it used to be", then you might like to ponder these extracts taken and adapted from newspaper reports of a 1920s fair, an occasion when a funeral had to take a tortuous route in order to dodge the crowd and to reach the parish church. Headed "Lament of older generation", it went on to report that: *"Times change and we with them, so one could hardly expect to find the Goose Fair... quite the counterpart of bygone years.*

Nevertheless there were elements about it that could have been noted a century back or more. True, the geese were conspicuous more by their absence than their presence, but the business of buying and selling was to be as much to the fore as ever.

The early morning mists, when the street lights twinkled cheerlessly under the coal restrictions, saw the itinerant vendors camped at their pitches, many of the former utilising their motor car or motor van as their shop window. [Is this how car boot sales originated?] Further along stalls were laden with sweetmeats and fairings of every variety, and away in the meadow by the river Tavy, the finishing touches were being put to the roundabouts and other fairground attractions.

One must not forget the hair-waving expert, nor the exhibitor of the working tin mine, the cutter of glass, the dispenser of 'really good razors', and the gentleman who, opposite the Cattle Market Inn, gave a scientific lecture on the stropping of those useful instruments.

In front of the mass of parked cars that filled the Guildhall Square, the semicircle of 'fairings' stalls effervesced with activity. The ever-thickening crowds were meticulous in keeping open traffic through the Square, not perhaps so much on account of wheeled traffic as for the herds of cattle, which without warning, other than a shout from the drover, lumbered through in columns of four – or as near as made no difference – at a brisk rate.

More geese were eaten in the cook-houses, restaurants, and hotels than were displayed for sale, and 'cheap jacks' largely displaced the farmer, who in older times offered his cattle and sheep to the highest bidders; but it still met the description of it in the directory, 'a fair for the sale of horses, cattle – and pleasure'.

Tavistock on Goose Fair Day is one vast bartering shop. You can buy anything from a 60 guineas [£63] shire horse down to a 10s [50 pence] sucker pony; from clothing down to fish and chips; from boots and harnesses down to goldfish. Cheapjacks offered an even greater variety than that, and they proffered their goods with a flood of oratory which many found irresistible. The town was full of swarthy men and women, unmistakably birds of passage.

During the forenoon the greatest animation was to be found in the cattle market. There were 2,000 head of sheep. Generally speaking the supply was greater than the demand and the prices were not high being a lot less than they were a month ago.

The horses and the Dartmoor ponies were accommodated in the road leading up to the downs. It was in the midst of all this sea of livestock that the few live geese reared their heads and betrayed their presence. They were objects of much interest. And so the day wore on. Tavistock Hospital Ambulance, complete with two 'patients', dispensed little red cross flags, and the Oakdale Colliery Band, from South Wales, enlivened proceedings and passed around collecting boxes outside Lloyd's Bank.

Dusk and evening brought the crudely picturesque lighting effects of the fair, etched in charcoal and yellow against the familiar buildings. Beneath flaming naphtha flares in the Square, keen-faced young men became hoarse in the selling of their wares. One cheapjack sported a top hat bedecked with £1 treasury notes. The crowd jostled each other in good humour. Only one case of drunkeness was seen – a woman who got to the station with great difficulty.

Plunging through the comparative darkness of Plymouth Road one came upon the entrance to the Wharf, where several supposedly Oriental ladies undertook to peer into matrimonial or financial futures... 'The Fat Lady' was a reminder of another feature of fairs that is dying out ... Perhaps the most popular of all the entertainments were the spinning wheels, where one bought a ticket, waited ten minutes for others do the same, pressed a switch and saw someone on the opposite side walk off with a huge fur 'Wilfred' or an alarm clock. There were several of these attractions...

And then homeward, while, behind, the several strident noises merged into one symphony of uproar gradually growing less. The night sky behind was a glare of light and rolling clouds of smoke, like an allegorical picture of the city of the damned. And directly above and ahead the clear cold pin points of the stars, and a clean wind from the moors. Another Goose Fair day, come and gone."

In various papers of that year it was reported that this might well be the last Goose Fair as most of the old-time customs had lapsed, this being one forecast that would prove to be completely wrong as we all now know. The one constant is that everyone one seems to fondly remember less commercialised Goose Fair days but, as this shows, in part, times do change but the memory is often selective in remembering only what it wants to – sunny days, outstanding characters and good times.

Do you speak English or do you speak 'Devonshire' or are you bilingual? If you are a visitor to these shores or parts you may as well give up now in trying to make sense out of these words of the Goose Fair song, but if you are aware of the accent and the phonetics then you will see what the traditional visit to the Fair entailed. Here are the words of the 1912 published version.

Tavvystock Goozey Fair
Tes just a month cum Vriday nex' Bill Champernown an' me
Us druv' a crost ole Dartymoor th' Goozey Vair to zee.
Us made our-sels quite 'vitty'
Us shav'd and grais'd our 'air
An' off us goes in our Zunday cloes behind Bill's ole grey mare.
Us smell'd the sage an' onions arl th' way fr'm Whitchurch Down,
An' didn' us av a blaw-out when us put up in th' town,
And theer us met Ned 'Annafurd, Jan Steer an' Nicky Square,
Ut sim to we arl Deb'm must be to Tavvystock Goozey Vair.
Chorus:
An' uts Aw thun, whur be'e gwaine, an' wot be'e doin of there?
'Aive down yer prong, an' stap down long, tes Tavvystock Goozey Vair.
Us went an' zeed th' osses, an' th' yaffers, an' the yaws,
Us went 'pun arl th' round-a-bouts an' in ter arl th' shaws
An' then ut started rainin'
'an blawin' too, Es Fai,
So off us goes back to th' 'Rose' an' 'aves a dish o' tay
An' then us 'ad a zing-zong an' th' folks kep' drappin in.
An' them wot knaw'd us arl came roun' an' 'ad a drap o' gin
Till wot with one an' t'other
Us didn' sim to care
Whether us wor to Bellevur Tor er Tavvystock Goosey Vair
(Chorus)
Twus rainin' in straims an' dark as pitch when us started 'ome that night
An' when us got pas' Merrivale Bridge th' mare er tuk a vright.
Says I to Bill, "Be careful er you'll av us in th' drains"
Says Bill ter me, "Be gad," says 'e, "Why, ab'm yew got th' reins?"
Just then th' mare run slap agin a whackin' gurt big stoan
'Er kicked th' trap to flibbits and 'er trotted off alone.
When us cum to us reckin'd twarn't no gude settin' there
So us 'ad to trudge 'ome thurteen mile fr'm Tavvystock Goosey Vair.
(Chorus)
So there you have it! For those bamboozled by the spelling, the dialect and the grammar, here is a simple interpretation.

About a month ago the unnamed narrator, and his friend, Bill Champernoun, took a day off from their agricultural employment and, smartened up for the occasion, set off to enjoy a day out at Tavistock Goosie Fair. Their mode of conveyance was a trap pulled by a wily grey mare, ultimately a more fortunate relation of the one featured in Widecombe Fair's song. As they approached the town from Whitchurch Down they caught a whiff of sage and onions on the breeze. In the first instance they had a Dartmoor farmer's-sized meal. Their appetites satisfied, they went and saw the various animals being sold, these being the horses, heifers, and ewes. The pair next visited the stalls and enjoyed the various attractions whilst the weather, no respecter of special days like this, had turned to rain and a strong wind had whipped up. By now the duo had cultivated an awesome thirst. This was quenched at the Rose where considerable amounts of tea and time were consumed. Whilst there old and familiar faces kept popping in, so much so that the lively assembly were soon in full voice singing, with great enthusiasm, the well-known tried and tested songs of the era. Once their thirsts had been quenched the gin bottle was 'consulted'. Our two friends enjoyed a boisterous time but well into the evening knew they had to begin their long journey home over the high moors. They noted that the weather was still awful, the wind was blowing strongly and the rain was pouring down but in their state of advanced inebriation it really didn't matter too much to them. The grey mare knew the way home but at Merrivale Bridge, some four miles on the journey back, misfortune overtook the woozy wayfarers. Each of them had thought that the other was holding the reins but neither was and, just as they realised this, the horse collided with a rock which demolished the cart and freed the mare from her taxi duties. She didn't wait around and strolled off into the night. Somewhat dazed, the Dartmoor duo were quite philosophical about their plight; realising that it was no good waiting there they set off to walk the thirteen miles home. Now you know!

For many years Mary Warne ran the Royal Standard, a pub at Mary Tavy. She had picked up the original and full version of the song from an old man who used to sing it whilst stood in front of a roaring fire at the Peter Tavy Inn. It became something of a party piece for her and was always well received.

Surprisingly there is no reference in the song to the goose dinners which were served up in a great many establishments in the town, people often paying over the odds for such a meal. Even then there were some cunning cooks who would get in a supply of rabbits, bleach them and then cook them in goose fat. These were then sold as cut-price goose dinners!

A Tavistock Town Trail

So what's left to do in exploring the town of Tavistock? Plenty! Hopefully this short walk around the town will reach the parts of the town's history that we haven't featured yet.

The route can be followed on this old 1906 map, which shows that the basic layout of the town remains the same but, as you will be able to see from matching it with reality, "Things ain't what they used to be!" I hope you have a head for heights!

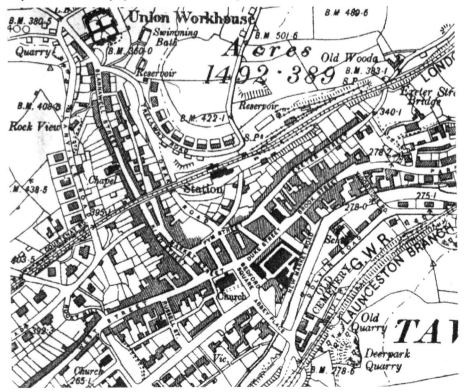

We begin in Bedford Square, close to the Tourist Information Centre, as it's the heart of Tavistock and easily found for those visiting the town for the first time. The Guildhall car park, used by people 'nipping' into Tavistock for a short visit, is the home of the seventh Duke of Bedford's fine statue, unveiled in the presence of some 2,000 spectators on 10 August 1864.

Head across the wide road of Bedford Square, bearing to the right of the church. On this central junction turn left into West Street.

The Corn Market, on the corner where West Street is joined by King Street, on the right, is a solid and attractive building that was built in the 1830s, on the former site of the Green Dragon, and at the instigation of the sixth Duke of Bedford. It was a corn market for some forty years, at a time when Tavistock was something of a boom town. This was an era when the many mines in the area generated a lot of trade. However, imports and a slump saw its decline and demise. In 1912 it became a picture palace but in the 1950s closed because of dwindling

audiences and competition from television. In 1958 it was again converted, this time to shops.

Tavistock also had another cinema, the Carlton, which was just along Russell Street, the next turning left along West Street. This is now a snooker hall but the town does have a cinema/theatre. 'The Wharf' is located, as you might have guessed, at the old canal wharf, and this house of entertainment has a much more modern look about it, a real asset to the town and this part of West Devon.

But as this is a town trail and not a 'film night' we had better stroll on along West Street. Just beyond the junction with Russell Street we leave this rising road by turning right, at the bottom of Rocky Hill, to ascend the unnamed Town Steps (known originally as 'the Tunnel') and enjoy some good uphill strolling.

At the top of this pedestrian thoroughfare there are three granite posts. The story sometimes told is that they were placed after an incident in October 1868. An active spinster ascended the lane only to look up in amazement as a bullock came charging down the slope towards her. Her sprightliness served her well for she turned into the line of fire and nimbly sidestepped into a recess allowing the creature to pass onwards and downwards. The granite posts appeared soon afterwards to stop repeats of the episode, so you shouldn't suffer the same fate! Pass between them and turn right.

We have now climbed to the gentler level of Glanville Road but we do not have to go all the way along this thoroughfare. A signpost, on the right, soon points us from the former railway bridge, spanning the line, down to the viaduct which once carried it. Although it is only a brief flirtation with one of the former railway lines to reach Tavistock, it shows the even trackbed needed for locomotives. Even if you are not a railway buff (or old buffer) you will find this elevated spot an interesting one for it gives a superb view of the town, even better, perhaps, then climbing the dizzy heights of the much more claustrophobic church tower, now well below to the right. This line, which saw a dozen deaths in its building, was originally created by the London and South Western Railway (LSWR) which arrived in the town some years after the Great Western Railway (GWR), the opposition. Tavistock thus had two stations, and two railways, one on each side of the valley.

At the end of the viaduct the path bears right in front of some modern dwellings to reach 'Tavistock North' railway station, now a private building and one guarded by alsatians. Having glimpsed 'Beeching's Folly', as it is now known, turn around and follow the road down the slope

under one of the arches of the viaduct to reach a junction. Although we turn left here, the former Tavistock Union Workhouse can be seen just up the hill on the right hand side. The late Tavistock window cleaner and part-time undertaker, Edgar J. C. Foot, used to tell the story of how John Lee, who was famous as "The Man They Couldn't Hang", tried to get into the workhouse to have a night's shelter but arrived too late and too drunk. He decided to climb the railings which then surrounded the buildings but slipped off them and fell heavily into soft ground. Stuck there and undiscovered, he may have reflected on an amazing career as his life ebbed away. He had cheated the hangman, James Berry, many years earlier but this further drop now proved fatal! Edgar Foot was involved in his funeral. If this story is true then it clears up a mystery that has baffled many people for years, most folks thinking Lee died in Canada, or Australia or the North-East of England. Lee's cheating of the hangman at Exeter Prison and the whole murder story surrounding him makes compelling reading. The full account of his 'execution' is featured in *Murders & Mysteries in Devon* by Ann James.

The road which lies downhill to our left, and once more under the viaduct, is Drake Road. It was forged, at its bottom end, through a line of buildings when the railway arrived in town. This provided the access needed to get to the new station. The narrow alley known as Post Office Lane, Mrs Fuge's refreshment establishment and some of the *Tavistock Gazette*'s premises were 'lost' in forging this route. However, just before we get there you may notice the previously mentioned Ordulph Arms on your right in Pym Street.

The imposing Town Council Offices and the Museum are found under the same roof on what is now our left side of Drake Road, just before it reaches Bedford Square. We carry on down the hill to reach Bedford Square where we turn left into Duke Street, a name that needs no further explanation.

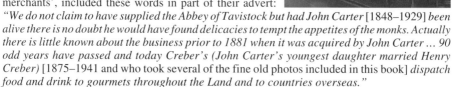

Tavistock is a fine shopping centre and draws on a large, predominantly rural, catchment area, many people preferring to shop here rather than in larger, impersonal, centres. There are a number of family businesses still trading here, Creber's being one of the best examples. This business trades from premises on the corner of Market Road, just where the level Duke Street runs into the equally flat Brook Street. In the 'souvenir catalogue' published in 1974 to celebrate 'The Tavistock Millennium' Creber's, 'The quality grocer – cheesemongers, pepperers, provision and wine merchants', included these words in part of their advert:

"We do not claim to have supplied the Abbey of Tavistock but had John Carter [1848–1929] been alive there is no doubt he would have found delicacies to tempt the appetites of the monks. Actually there is little known about the business prior to 1881 when it was acquired by John Carter ... 90 odd years have passed and today Creber's (John Carter's youngest daughter married Henry Creber) [1875–1941 and who took several of the fine old photos included in this book] dispatch food and drink to gourmets throughout the Land and to countries overseas."

John Carter was noted for his kindness to the poorer members of the community, having had a humble background himself when growing up. He had worked at Wheal Maria before becoming involved with this firm. Creber's have had various 'firsts' in their trading at Tavistock having introduced frozen foods in 1946 and sherry 'from the wood' in 1962, the word 'quality' being their hallmark. Long may they continue! These pictures show the shop in various periods of its development on and around the same site.

The Tavistock Inn is on the left hand side of the street and it is unusual to have an inn bearing the town's name in the place itself. There is a Tavistock Inn at Poundsgate on Dartmoor, on the road to Tavistock, which is more usual. After all, there are many Exeter Inns (there used to be one in Tavistock!) but none in the county town itself and the same may be said of Plymouth! Tavistock's very own Tavistock Inn was originally a private house. However, one of its Victorian residents, John Richards, started a brewery on land behind the pub. This venture was successful, peaking in its output in the early 1920s when it brewed more than half a million pints of ale per year, more than enough for one almighty hangover! Like many smaller breweries it was subsequently bought out and closed down, this being just another takeover in this predatory industry. The building has been a pub since 1894.

Just as we approach a large garden centre, formerly the Old Town Mill, we turn right to cross the narrow Vigo Bridge, which bears the plaque shown in the picture. Looking upstream it's possible to see the much more recent Stannary Bridge built to reduce the town centre's traffic flow.

This bridge spans the Tavy, a wonderful river which starts on the high peat plateau of Northern Dartmoor. It then plunges more than a thousand feet in seven miles to rush on past, through, and sometimes into, Tavistock. It then loops and twists its way through a deep wooded valley to enter its shortened estuary before mingling its waters with the Tamar near Bere Ferrers. *Along The Tavy* is a journey along it from source to mouth and the 'bits' on Tavistock are not a repeat of what is in this book.

We now turn right and if wasn't for the traffic we might be forgiven for thinking that we were in Victorian times once more, for the cottages and school building of St Rumon's Infants' School along Dolvin Road, and the graveyard opposite, are pure nineteenth century in their external appearance. It's a long narrow cemetery with various larger chambers built into the hillside, reminiscent of the catacombs built into Exeter's Roman wall. It is not at all a morbid experience to browse the epitaphs here for even those cut short in their prime would have passed their 'sell by' date long before now, most of the 'residents' having been laid to rest between the 1830s and '80s. Some of the epitaphs reflect the toughness of life in Victorian times, recording deaths in the local mines or in the building of the railways to the town. The route of the GWR railway from Tavistock South towards Lydford passed across the top of this cemetery whilst the river, another cause of several deaths, was almost as close just beyond Dolvin Road.

In no time at all Tavistock's Abbey Bridge is soon reached; the crossing, an effortless one, brings you back to the start where the Duke of Bedford casts a watchful eye over your safe return. I wonder what he thought when he peered down on the visiting rugby team, many years ago, who were full of high spirits. In their midst was the Rev Pratt, a keen and accomplished rugby player who became the Vicar of nearby Peter Tavy. He was in the habit of sporting a battered broad-brimmed black trilby. However, as his team got off their coach in Bedford Square it was rudely removed from his head and after a passing movement was the victim of an immense kick, from a point close to the Duke's statue all the way to the churchyard opposite. Whilst the rugby players sought a pub for a beer or twelve the good vicar went in search of his hat and was spotted the next day with it relocated on his head. Those who were of a disposition to take a close look at it noticed there were several fresh stitches in the heavily patched and repaired trilby.

This book is deliberately and ambiguously titled *Around & About Tavistock* because it looks at the town and its setting. Around it is some of the best country-side in Devon, and on its doorstep is a delightful village which has had an identity crisis when establishing itself as a separate entity.

Whitchurch is located on the former main road to Plymouth. However, in 1822 a new route was forged, details of which are included in one of the sister books to this one, *Around & About Roborough Down*. It is now joined, in urban wedlock, to Tavistock, both places having spread over green fields to unite, and this extract confirms that this spread began quite some time ago!

The Book of Fair Devon, published in 1900, had this to say of Whitchurch: "*...a typical moorland village, is pleasantly situated on the fringe of Whitchurch Down. There is reason to believe that a church existed here of pre-Norman times. The present church was restored a few years ago. A large number of new houses have been built along the road to Tavistock, and there are still many excellent building sites available, overlooking the valley of the Tavy. There are several old mansions including Walreddon, which was long a seat of the Courtenays; Halwell, where the Granvilles resided for three centuries before removing to Kilworthy, in the parish of Tavistock; and Grenofen, belonging to the Chichesters. On the Down is a fine example of an ancient cross known as the 'Pixie's Cross'.*" This massive cross, also referred to by some as 'Monks', which has a rugged, unfinished look about it, is the subject of an old story. In the seventeenth century, at the time of the Commonwealth, a new parson was appointed at Whitchurch and soon set to work to sweep away superstitions, false idols and anything to detract from Puritan worship. The Pixie's Cross became a focus of attention for him but perhaps he should have left it well alone!

He suggested to his fellow parishioners that they should remove it but they would have no part in it. Therefore he felt obliged to sort the situation himself. At the cross he suddenly became aware of a menacing presence behind him in the shape of a large bull. Unable to bolt to the nearest 'sanctuary' all he could do was to mount the cross and hope that the creature would soon tire and leave. But this was not the case and all day and all night the two kept each other company.

At daybreak a little old lady, bound for market at Tavistock, appeared out of the gloom. She was astonished at what she thought she saw at Pixie's Cross. In the poorest of light she discerned the Devil, no less, sat atop the cross whilst at its base was his sidekick, a monstrous, four-legged and horned creature. She did what most would do in that situation and ran, as fast as her legs would carry her, down into Whitchurch. However, in the interlude the gloom lifted and the 'brave' Whitchurch villagers who came to witness the Devil were amused to see their preacher cowering on the top of Pixie's Cross. He bade them scare off the bull but they had the presence of mind to negotiate the keeping of the cross in its rightful place. The vicar was hardly in a position to argue and Pixie's Cross remains a landmark to wayfarers crossing the down. Just how much of that story is fact or fiction we don't know but there are probably a few grains of truth in it.

The church of St Andrew, on the lane leading up to Whitchurch Down, is the last resting place of a famous person, an Antipodean adventurer and hero. It couldn't be any more different to the hot, dry interior of Australia, a world, or half at least, away from where he made a lasting name for himself. General Edward John Eyre (1815–1901), the son of a Yorkshire parson, is the same person whose surname will be found in good atlases because the geographical features of Lake Eyre and the Eyre Peninsular are named after him. Lake Eyre, in South Australia, which the general visited in 1840, is a little bigger than Devon.

He arrived in Australia at the age of eighteen and, as a sheep farmer, built a reputation for himself as a protector of the aborigines. However, he suffered from wanderlust and in a country the size of Australia there was always going to be an excess of opportunity awaiting the young man. After a few sedentary years he followed in the footsteps of other explorers, his mission being to seek an overland route for driving cattle to Albany in western Australia. In June 1840 he set out on an epic journey from Adelaide with a fellow white man and three black boys. However Eyre's white companion was murdered by two of the natives who ran off with the bulk of the expedition's food. Eyre had no choice other than to continue. A year after having set out on his epic journey across the great, virtually waterless, expanse fate eventually smiled on him and the sole surviving aborigine. They were rescued by the crew of a French whaling ship. Despite the privations of this journey, freshly victualled, he was able to complete the first east-to-west crossing of southern Australia.

The well-travelled General was regarded as a tough but fair-minded character who, whilst in his post as Governor of Jamaica, was suspended from duty for his adjudged harsh handling of a black riot in 1865. He settled back to a quieter life at nearby Walreddon, about a mile to the south west of Whitchurch, where he was known for his kindness.

Within the same graveyard is the sad epitaph of Mary Metters who was brutally murdered with a billhook, in February 1816, by her servant Sam Norton, a man with a previous criminal record. Mary's husband, having given him employment, had thought that Norton was a reformed character, but this turned out to be a fatal error of judgement.

The Whitchurch Inn, beside the church, was originally the Church House Inn, an apt name. There are many with such a name still today, Stoke Gabriel, Harberton and Torbryan all having 'Church House Inns', to name but some of the many in Devon. When country journeys to church were on foot it was necessary to cater for church-goers. This inn fulfilled that role and, following a church service, those with a long way to walk home could be fed and watered.

As a teenager I can remember scaling some of the dizzy heights of the tors on the western side of Dartmoor, vantage points like Cox Tor and Pew Tor, that overlook the Tavistock and Whitchurch area. Way below was a complex of regimentally-spaced buildings that covered a considerable area and it was only in later years, long after the site had been cleared, that I discovered that this was the military camp known as Plaster or Plaister Down. In 1943 it was developed as a military hospital (115th Station Hospital) for American troops. Following the D-Day landings there was an influx, by train, of sick and injured men. The American presence in the district was great, as all manner of buildings were commandeered by them and one of the church halls was taken over to become the US post office. It's believed that the whole of what is now the golf course on Whitchurch Down was covered in tents, a place where black and white American servicemen were segregated. There was an impressive nucleus of buildings, a virtual self-contained small town complete with cinema, equipped with some 1,500 seats salvaged from a blitzed Plymouth cinema, and a variety of shops. Many Americans befriended local girls and, following the end of the war, there was an exodus of not only American troops but also an army of local brides accompanying them.

But that wasn't quite the end of the story for Plaster Down was to see a procession of different types of personnel passing through, many resentful at the harshness of the weather experienced here in winter time. Polish refugees, German prisoners of war, the Territorials, the Women's Royal Army Corps, the Army, the Royal Marines and almost everyone except Uncle Tom Cobley and co seemed to pass through as the camp changed its function every few years.

In the latter part of 1972 the camp accommodated some 600 Ugandan Asians, of the 49,000 expelled by Idi Amin. No doubt they noticed the contrast in climate more than most!

There was much discussion between 1973 and 1975 as to what to do with the camp, but the debate ended in 1976 when it was demolished, conspicuous water tower and all. The closure had an impact on the town's economy because many locals had derived employment or trade from it.

Whitchurch Down is a fine place to walk and many take advantage of the lack of steep gradients and the good ground conditions found over much of this extensive down.

Another book, the award-wining *Wheelchair Walks in Devon* by Lucinda Ruth Gardner, includes a walk along part of the Tavistock Canal, a watercourse whose history is entwined with the town where it started and which gave it its name. To walk beside it, almost but not quite as far as Morwell Tunnel, makes for a pleasant, easy jaunt, the perfect excuse to explore the country just to the south and west of the town. For those who want to know more of this area and its past I have included a little history, spiked with snippets of trivia, to make for a more meaningful meander along the canal banks.

The one real joy of canal walking is that the route follows level ground, and in a hilly area like the one surrounding Tavistock this has to be a real bonus. However, for those who hanker after hills the walk can be extended, and full details have been included in case you have the necessary stamina to explore further the countryside surrounding Tavistock.

The engineering of the Tavistock Canal, by mining genius John Taylor, was a skilful operation. The Tavy, a fast, steeply-profiled river, was of little use for navigation. The smallest of boats could not travel beyond its estuary so Tavistock was virtually landlocked. By building this $4^1/_2$-mile-long canal Tavistock became linked to the navigable Tamar at the river port of Morwellham, the canal ending some 240 feet high above the quays. To complete the link an incline railway was constructed to carry cargoes up (or down) the steep slope from the banks of the Tamar. This, and much more, can be seen on a visit to the tourist attraction of Morwellham Quay, which brings the mining history and Victorian atmosphere of the area to life.

The 'imports', which included coal, lime and foodstuffs, were brought up to Tavistock in horse-drawn iron barges. Going down to Morwellham the 'exports' included copper ore, slate and granite, and within a short time of opening the canal was carrying about 20,000 tons of goods each year. However, today those same canal waters are only used to generate hydro-electric power at Morwellham, and a visit to the small HEP plant is part of the visit to the river port.

Our walk begins from Bedford Square, once again at the Duke of Bedford's statue, simply because it's an easy place for visitors to find and is not far from the start of the Tavistock Canal. Cross the road to the Abbey Bridge and, without crossing it, descend to walk beside the river. On your left is the Tavy, complete with weirs, and no doubt someone fishing, and on your right a tall wall. The canal's waters are taken from a point just below the bridge but the start of the canal here is not seen. Follow the river and at the third 'gap' in the wall turn right into the car park. The Wharf Cinema (Theatre/Entertainment Centre) is in front of you. Bear left towards the leisure centre and steer to the right of it making sure not to plunge headlong into the shallow canal. Route instructions now become unnecessary for all you have to do, for the next few miles, is follow the

Tavistock Canal, your personal guide and companion on this stroll.

Today's junk can become tomorrow's treasures. There were just nine 'Robey Tandem Rollers' manufactured and one once stood in the former play park where the leisure centre is now located. From 1962 this old vehicle, courtesy of the town council, was placed here for children to enjoy. This inanimate object was christened 'Stumbles the Steam-roller', an unofficial name which 'she' has never displayed on any nameplate. However, various collectors of such venerable vehicles regarded such a

Around & About Tavistock

plaything as something worthy of better use. Somebody said of her presence that it was like "Using a Rolls-Royce for a chicken coop in the backyard!" and after the ravages of twenty years of use and misuse she was taken from the Meadows. Eleven years of restoration followed and an incredible amount of money, time, love and attention was lavished on her to bring her back to pristine condition. Now she is taken out on special occasions, and is the pride and joy of those who laboured so hard and long to restore her to her former glory.

The canal runs a straight course here. To the left is the Meadows Park, formerly Jessop's Hay Meadow, and, beyond the canal, to the right the tennis courts stand on what was Frog Meadow, a name lapsed into local amphibian folklore. Stay with the canal to a point close to West Bridge which spans the Tavy. Here the main road has to be crossed.

The grey and imposing Fitzford Gate, rebuilt in 1871, is found close to Drake's Statue and its colour is a good match for its reputation as being a spot once inhabited by a scheming lady. We have already heard of the infamous and much maligned Lady Howard who, although depicted in a number of oil paintings, was no oil painting! According to J. Henry Harris (1907): *"Fitzford Gate was the place where people settled their little differences in true Devonshire fashion, and the best man won. It was here that Sir John Fitz (the Hotspur of the time) slew his neighbour, Mr Slanning of Bickley* [sic]. *The quarrel arose out of some petty personal taunt, and could have been settled amicably, had not Sir John's second cried out 'What child's play; come to fight and now put up your sword!' Then swords flashed again, and Slanning, losing his balance through the hitching of his spur, received a lethal thrust. To tell a man that you will 'settle accounts' at Fitzford Gate is quite enough."*

Close to the canal are fine examples of Victorian workers', mainly miners', dwellings. On the east side of the River Tavy are the five terraces of Westbridge Cottages, built in 1850 and designed by Theophilus Jones, whilst near the canal are

the two rows of Fitzford Cottages. A closer inspection of these, or the other ducal cottages, would reveal that many bore coronets or the letter 'B' for Bedford. They were built following a cholera epidemic when the overcrowded town suffered from problems of 'piss-poor' (to use their phrase not mine!) public hygiene. Before Westbridge Cottages were built, it is believed that local sports-men took advantage of the flat site, on which they are built, using it as a cricket field. Today Tavistock's cricket club have the unusual but picturesque ground on Whitchurch Down, which we saw earlier.

Away to the right, but dominating the scene, is the immense structure of a church which might well have not remained a distinct Tavistock landmark had circumstances been a little different...

This enormous church, built at the behest of the eighth Duke of Bedford in 1867, might well have gone to pastures new. There was a genuine intent, in the late 1920s, to take this Henry Clutton-designed building apart and transport it to Exeter, where it would meet the demands of the St Marks district for a place of worship. Tavistock's St George's (Fitzford Church) was seen as the perfect solution. For some £13,000 Exeter could have this derelict building, the locals having voted by postcard, by an overwhelming 583 votes for, to just 119 against, to let it go. And so in earnest, Ernest Hooper, an eminent architect of his day, and the Rev J. A. Godfrey, Rector of St Mary Major, Exeter, visited Tavistock in great anticipation of completing a move. If lighthouses like Smeaton's Tower, now on Plymouth Hoe, had been successfully removed from the Eddystone Reef, why not move a church? Well, although God moves in mysterious ways, sometimes His 'houses' don't, and a close inspection told the architect that the shaly nature of the building would mean that most of it would be lost in dismantling. The plans were abandoned, the church remained redundant, until 1936, and St Marks got its own new redbrick-built church. If only the Rev Godfrey had lived long enough to see the irony; St George's is still there but his own massive church, St Mary Major, which stood directly in front of Exeter Cathedral, was demolished in 1974 and used as solid infill for a new housing development!

Although every church's history is well documented, it's interesting to note the chequered past of this one. It was opened in 1867 as a chapel-of-ease for the Anglican parish church and a place of worship for the mining community but, owing to a decrease in population, was closed in 1917. It was reopened, by the Bishop of Exeter, in 1936 after some £500 had been spent on it to bring it up to a usable condition. However, in the very cold year of 1947 it closed again. This time the Anglicans virtually gave it up as a lost cause, only for the Catholics to acquire it in 1952, and now it is the church of Our Lady of the Assumption.

The walk along the Tavistock Canal has much going for it as it's easy on the feet, flat (something quite rare in Devon), and soon takes the walker into glorious countryside. But first it has to pass between the Community College's massive complex of buildings and a set of allotments, some bearing ramshackle sheds which do not enhance the scenery. These corrugated sheds give way to new housing on the west bank. When I did this walk there was a distinct smoky haze surrounding several pupils standing on the bank of the canal who, rather than appreciating a fine feat of engineering, were enjoying a sly cigarette. The canal turns away from 'civilisation' into a wooded corridor running just above the flood plain of the River Tavy. A disused quarry is soon passed as the path heads on to the site where one of the world's great Elizabethans made his first appearance.

Crowndale was the birthplace of Drake but there are no remains of the dwelling where he was born; the one passed today is much more recent. The information board just beyond Crowndale reveals all. To the right, and up the slope will be seen the former railway which ran from Tavistock North to Bere Alston and on into Plymouth, but we'll meet it again later and more than once! If you have canoed to this point you will need to heed the signs regarding your immediate options.

Our route on 'terra firma' continues ever onward along the towpath beneath trees. The flat valley floor of the Tavy becomes increasingly farther below us because, whilst we keep to higher ground, the river is dropping all the while. Beside it is the Crowndale Recycling Centre, but it clearly doesn't extend to recycling its own appearance into something more attractive or environmentally easy-on-the-eye! We continue to a point at Shillamill where the tributary valley of the River Lumburn joins the Tavy. The canal turns right to follow the contour, taking the walker under the towering structure of Shillamill Viaduct where canoeists can go no farther. When the railway was being built there was a community of navvies living here in what can only be described, by current standards, as the most basic accommodation. No doubt they worked long hours and spent little time in their crude huts.

Today it's only possible to travel by train from Plymouth as far as Bere Alston, which is a great pity for had the line remained open through to Tavistock it would have provided an excellent alternative journey for many of those who now

commute to Plymouth each working day. Such a relaxing rail journey along the Tamar would be surely preferable to the stop/go rush hour traffic from Tavistock through Plymouth's ever-growing suburbs, and on into the city centre. More about this line can be discovered in another of my books *Railways on and around Dartmoor*.

About 100 yards beyond the viaduct is an enormous fallen tree spanning the canal. Fortunately a way has been cut through to enable walkers to progress.

The penknives have been out along this section and tree graffiti are evident along the next stretch. Eventually the path, and canal, make a sharp turn left onto another example of engineering endeavour. This is the Lumburn Aqueduct which carried the canal over the River Lumburn. Just beyond it you will discover that, although the canal carries on to its great tunnel through Morwell Down, you won't be there to see it enter this twilight world. Your canal caper is curtailed by a somewhat inebriated sign and a stout gate, courtesy of Tavistock Woodlands Sawmill, at nearby Gulworthy. All I can do is tell you about it. Morwell Tunnel was the major stumbling block in the completion of the canal because it took some fourteen years to build. However, when it was finished,

there was a great sense of achievement. The canal, which had been estimated to cost £36,958, approximately, had run up a tab of almost twice that amount. The tunnel, a staggering $1^3/_4$ miles long, was cited as one of the major reasons for the spiralling cost. It's hard to picture the scene, almost two centuries ago, when it was officially opened. This is how it was reported: *"At 8 o'clock some 400 gaily decorated persons of all ranks entered nine of the small iron boats. The whole party proceeded in the aquatic subterranean excursion with the grandest order and regularity and prepared to take leave of daylight for about two hours."* The report went on to relate that some of the more nervous passengers derived comfort from the strains of the various local bands who accompanied the procession as they passed, at one point, some 360 feet beneath the summit of Morwell Down. There was both relief and excitement as eventually the procession emerged from the darkness into the bright sunlight on the Morwellham side of the tunnel. Here some 5,000 spectators had assembled to watch the spectacle. A 21-gun salute was fired from vessels moored at the quays and, to complete the proceedings, there was dancing, refreshments and toasts made to the appropriate persons and organisations involved.

Beyond the tunnel lies the major tourist attraction and educational resource of Morwellham Quay on the navigable River Tamar, a place that all should visit at some time, and here, by following one of the trails, it's possible to see the other end of the tunnel. A day spent listening to the audio-visual shows, walking along the trails and visiting all the parts and places to be seen will teach you more about the Victorian river port than any book.

There was a link to the Tavistock Canal which came in from the north at the point where we are now standing. This was the Millhill Cut, a short waterway to the numerous quarries in and around the hamlet of Millhill. Today it's just a dry ditch and the photograph I took of it, for posterity, must rank as about the most boring one I have ever taken!

You have a choice. You can either retrace your steps back to Tavistock or, if you are fit and healthy and game for some lanes and hills, you might like to do the moderately enjoyable walk that I did. If so, read on!

Cross the concrete bridge over the canal and go through the gate onto the track, this being the towpath of the Millhill Cut. Again we are skirting the Lumburn valley as we head northwards to reach the main road between Tavistock and Gunnislake at the hamlet called Lumburn. A century ago there was a corn mill on the west side of the river and an iron and brass foundry on the east bank. Turn right along this busy highway and take extreme care to stay in single file along the verge, which soons gives up on you. You will only need to stay with the road for the shortest of distances because a turn-off, to the left, is encountered almost immediately. This is signed to 'Newton'. Follow this road uphill, the start of a long and steady climb. Initially the surface is clean but when farm buildings are encountered it is embellished with the trade marks of agricultural pursuits... At the first fork, at pebble-dashed, double-glazed 'Newton', bear right on the higher road. At this point you can look backwards to views of Dartmoor, the tall thin landmark of North Hessary Tor's mast visible in the distance.

The road continues to climb to reach a junction at Colcharton where this relic of the area's industrial past is embedded in the hedge. Turn right towards Millhill, the gradient is now less demanding. The road passes 'Toad Hall' with a sign featuring an amiable amphibian sitting on a rock. Soon the highest point on this walk is reached and the lane begins to level out before dropping down into the Lumburn valley once more. Ahead are the Millhill Quarries and beside the river, on its west bank is the small settlement of Millhill. This mining and quarrying hamlet had a certain symmetry in its layout with its 24 'Duke of Bedford' cottages, these being arranged in six clusters of four. This mild form of regimentation extended, at least in Victorian times, to the gardens where the front ones, a floral picture postcard scene at the right time of the year, were lovingly tended by the ladies whilst the rear gardens resembled a scene from *The Good Life,* where enough fruit and vegetables were grown to see a small family through a year, cultivated by the menfolk. (I

would imagine things would be, and need to be, different today!) This home-grown produce was so important, in the heyday of the mining, with families living on a meagre income and shops some distance away. However, not far from here is another hamlet, Chipshop, a name with which

I feel a certain affinity! But this has nothing to do with takeaway food – part of a miner's wages were 'chips', these being tokens which could only be exchanged at the mine company's shop, the chip shop.

At the junction, just before Millhill, we turn away from the direction of Chipshop to go right and head back to Tavistock, some two miles distant. Although the last lanes were quiet this one back to the Stannary Town of Tavistock is much busier, so vehicle vigilance is necessary.

The Lumburn is crossed for the last time, at Middle Lumburn Bridge. Here there is a disused quarry, on the left, opposite the pink-washed Crease Cottage, a name which will be encountered several times because the lane to Tavistock is Crease Lane. At the next junction fork right and stay with this road all the way to Tavistock. It climbs high above the Lumburn and from the first gateway on the right the meandering river can be seen down below wending across its narrow valley floor.

Soon outer Tavistock is met, first with bungalows and a pavement on the right hand side of the road. The lane then starts to drop steeply to reach a bridge over the former railway, the one which we passed under earlier in the canal caper. Walk left down onto the line, where there are picnic tables if you need them, and head on into Tavistock. If you have walked the town trail you will know precisely how to get back to Bedford Square; if not, then read page 21 and this will tell you how to end the ramble on the right lines … and get back to where we started much earlier.

We have now completed our look at 'the most delightful town in West Devon'. We have met its tough 'guys and dolls', strolled around its streets, visited its viaduct, been a guest at Goose Fair, and sung its song. Tavistock is a sturdy town steeped in history, set in glorious countryside, the jewel in the crown of this corner of the county. I hope this little book will have whetted your appetite sufficiently for you to go and find out more about this ancient stannary town and its wonderful surrounding countryside.